In Their Own Words

In Their Own Words

CONVERSATIONS WITH YOUTH ABOUT THEIR FOSTER CARE EXPERIENCES AND WHAT WE CAN LEARN FROM THEM

Jim Bridges
PATHWAY CARING FOR CHILDREN

IN THEIR OWN WORDS
CONVERSATIONS WITH YOUTH ABOUT THEIR FOSTER CARE EXPERIENCES AND
WHAT WE CAN LEARN FROM THEM

In Their Own Words by Jim Bridges © 2012 by Pathway Caring for Children.
Edited by Velma Bridges.

Book design by Jessica Bennett.
In Their Own Words cover photograph, "Love Lasts forever," was photographed
by Innis Maggiore.

All rights reserved.

No part of this book may be reproduced, stored or transmitted in any
manner whatsoever—except in the case of brief quotations embodied in critical
articles and reviews—without written permission from
Pathway Caring for Children.

Printed in the United States of America by
Standard Printing Company
1115 Cherry Avenue NE
Canton, Ohio 44704

ISBN: 978-0-9856032-0-5

10 9 8 7 6 5 4 3 2 1

Pathway
Caring for Children

PATHWAY CARING FOR CHILDREN
4895 DRESSLER RD. NW, SUITE A
CANTON, OHIO 44718
WWW.PATHWAYCFC.ORG

This book is dedicated to foster and adopted children, and to all who choose to make a difference in the lives of these children.

The fired clay candle holder "Love Lasts Forever" on the front cover was handmade and painted for author Jim Bridges by a 12-year-old girl in Pathway's foster care program. Jim kept this candle holder on his desk or in a prominent place in his office. The photograph was taken by Innis Maggiore in Canton, Ohio, and used in their design for Pathway's 2002 Annual Report.

Contents

	FOREWORD	3
Chapter 1	INTRODUCTION	5
Chapter 2	BEGINNINGS	13
Chapter 3	THE HUNGER FOR FAMILY	21
Chapter 4	WHY DO THEY DO THAT?	31
Chapter 5	LIVING THROUGH THE PROBLEMS	43
Chapter 6	MOVING ON WITH LIFE	49
Chapter 7	ADVICE TO FOSTER PARENTS	57
Chapter 8	HOPE FOR THE FUTURE	65
	TRIBUTE TO THE AUTHOR	69

Foreword

It has been a number of years since my late husband, Jim Bridges, began talking with youth and young adults about their experiences in foster care. Jim really listened to these youth. He sought to give them a voice in this book for the purpose of improving the care of all foster children. When Jim died in 2009, this book had not yet been published. I knew that Jim had spent many hours working on this project with the great passion for children and youth that characterized all of his work. I wanted to do whatever was needed to complete the project. I wanted you to hear the voices of Lance and Leon, Samantha and Sarah, and of all the others. I wanted you to hear and learn from their stories.

It has been an honor for me to work with others who helped in the editing of this book. During the process, we have become convinced that these young people have much of great value to tell us. If we can see our children and youth through the lens of Jim's compassion and understanding, I believe we will be inspired to move forward with the important work of providing quality care for them. And so I invite you to truly listen to what Janet and Jeremy, Andrew and Adrianne, and many others have to say "In Their Own Words."

Velma Bridges

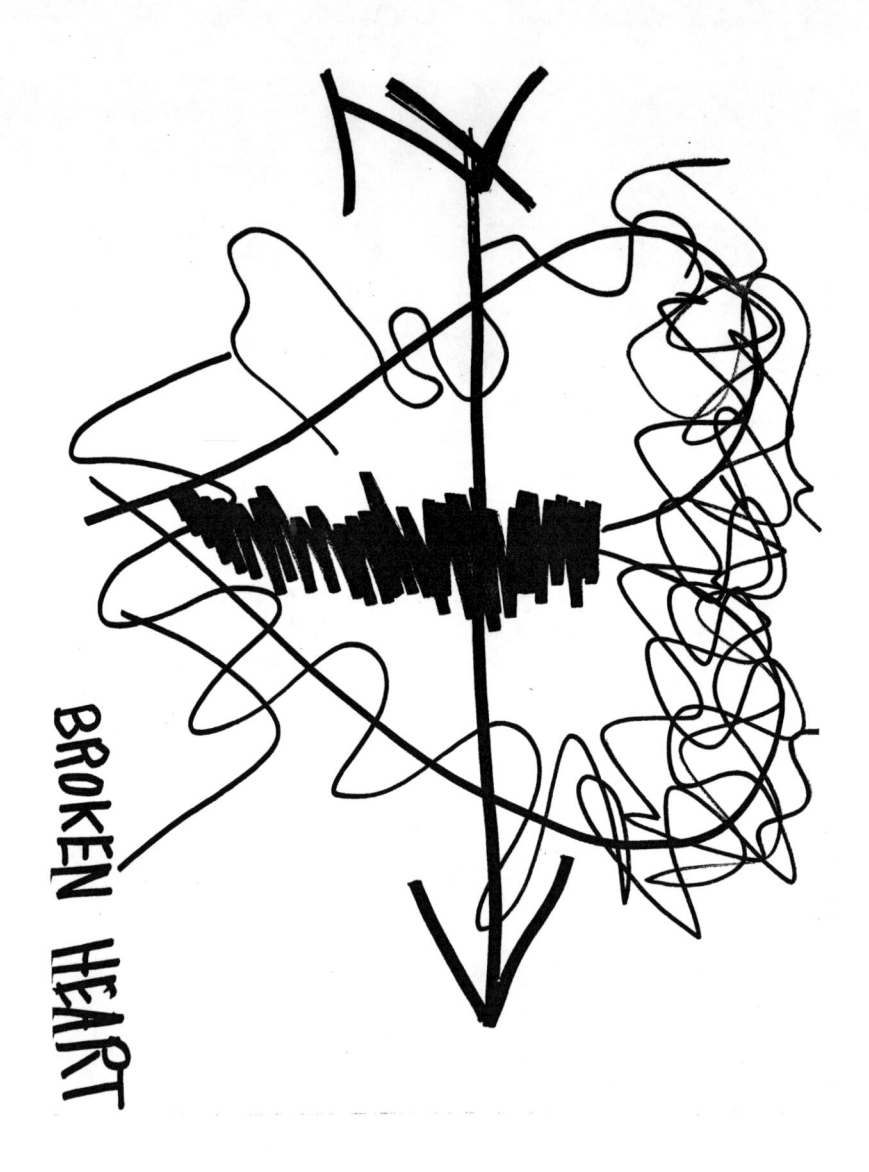

"BROKEN HEART PIERCED BY REJECTION" was drawn by a 9-year-old girl.

Chapter 1
Introduction

I have been talking to foster children for more than 30 years. Several years ago, I started listening to them. Really listening. In that process, I have learned much that I believe will help foster parents improve their parenting of these fragile children. That is the purpose of this book.

I have sought to give voice to foster children, whose voice often goes unheard as professionals plan for them, train others about them and make decisions for them.

This book began when I started recording interviews with children who wanted to talk with me about their experiences—good and bad—in foster care. After the interviews, I transcribed them, exactly as the kids spoke. I sought to capture their unique phraseology, their colloquialisms, their syntax, so it was really the kids who were speaking. As I became more and more involved in the project, I was increasingly aware that these children have some profound, often eloquent things to say to us. I wanted to let them say it—"In Their Own Words."

Each interview was conducted and recorded with the permission of the child. When it came time to include the interviews in this publication, I changed names and some details about the lives of the youth, so as to protect their privacy. Their comments remained, however, faithful to their thoughts and their unique ways of expressing them.

Perhaps a few words about the thinking of neglected, abused, and abandoned children are appropriate. Over the years, I have found a simple paradigm useful in understanding these children and how to intervene positively in their lives.

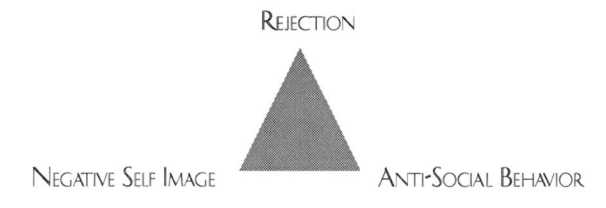

REJECTION

▲

NEGATIVE SELF IMAGE   ANTI-SOCIAL BEHAVIOR

At the apex of the triangle is the experience of rejection.

Adults looking at the families of children who have been neglected, abused, and abandoned understand that the parents often had overwhelming problems, which prevented them from giving care to their children. These problems include things like mental illness, physical disabilities, extreme poverty, lack of employable skills, and drug and alcohol addiction.

Almost all parents love their children and want the absolute best for them, but sometimes problems such as these interfere with this natural desire.

"MY STORY"—GEORGE

Here's how George describes the events leading up to his mother's abandonment of her children:

> *I was born in Texas and I ended up in quite a few different states. My mother really wasn't able to keep one place. The men that she was with lived in different cities, and we ended up with them for some reason. So, I guess we just ended up staying with the guys she liked, more or less.*
>
> *We were living in Garaway at the time. A couple of weeks after my youngest sister's birthday, our mom took off. Up and left us in the morning. She left everything behind, didn't leave a note or anything. I think she had my father or one of our relatives come pick her up. She ended up back in Texas. And the guy we were with reported it to the police and they took us to a foster home.*
>
> *I personally think she left us because she was not financially able to take care of us. Just about everywhere we went she tried to apply for food stamps. Unfortunately, we weren't able to get them, because she wasn't a resident of Ohio. You have to be a resident for six months before you can get food stamps. So she wasn't able to get them because we had just moved there for a few weeks.*

As he indicates here, George was eventually able, after extensive counseling, to understand that his mother abandoned him out of economic necessity. It was the only way she could find to solve the desperate problem of feeding her children. With help, many children can come to similar understanding.

At the time it happens, however, these children often see themselves as having been rejected by their parents because they were somehow defective. They believe that their removal from their parents' care is their fault. They tell themselves things like, "If I had not wet the bed, I would still be with Mom and Dad," and "If I hadn't spilt my milk so many times, this never would have happened."

This experience of rejection is a deep-down, inside-the-person feeling. It is not rational and reasonable by any adult standard. But it is real to the child who experiences it. These children describe themselves as feeling empty, hollow, confused, lonely, isolated, scared and sick.

I cannot forget the experience of taking some of our youth to a summer camp in North Carolina. In the group was a boy named Herman. He had a bright and engaging smile, but beneath the surface, he was seething with anger at the world around him.

It was not hard to tell where his anger was coming from. When he spoke about his life, he talked of being deserted by his father—who subsequently went to prison—and by his mother, who was addicted to drugs. His career in foster homes had involved so many placements that he had lost count. He told me once that he felt "like a dead letter that nobody wanted."

Herman's anger achieved expression through disrupting and causing problems for anyone and everyone around him. During the week at camp, he refused to participate in activities, disrupted meetings, and stole money from the pop machine.

In the middle of that week, however, Herman participated in a group in which I was also a participant. Each of us was instructed to take a paper bag. On the outside of the bag, we were asked to place pictures of the image that we showed to the world around us—what we wanted people to believe about us. On the inside of this bag, we were supposed to place pictures showing who we felt we really were. Then we were asked to show to other members of the group what we had put on the outside of our bags, as well as what we had placed inside the bags.

I watched anxiously as the other teenagers showed the outside and inside of their paper bags, wondering what Herman would do when it was his turn. I was ready for trouble. At last, Herman began to speak. He held up his bag and explained the pictures of men and women dressed in fancy clothes, drinking various alcoholic beverages, and driving sleek automobiles. This was truly the image that he wanted to portray to the world.

Then Herman took his bag, turned it over, and shook it. There was nothing! The bag was as empty as Herman felt himself to be.

This emptiness and alienation leads to the second leg of the triangle—the development of a negative self-image.

The neglected, abused, or abandoned child looks around at other children he knows in his neighborhood, his school, his church or his scout pack. He sees that they are happily living with one or both of their parents. He says to himself, "There must be something wrong with me because I can't live with my family." This is the beginning of a negative self-image, an overwhelming feeling of worthlessness and valuelessness. From it springs messages to oneself of "I am nothing, no one. I'll never be anyone or do anything." One child described her feelings this way:

"I WAS JUST LIKE NOTHING"—JANET

> *I felt like no one wanted me, that I was just like nothing to anyone. I didn't mean anything, I had no point in life, I had no meaning to be here or exist.*

Out of such a feeling often comes behavior that creates problems for those around the child. Sociologists sometimes call this anti-social behavior, and it is represented by the third leg of the triangle. The behaviors range from withdrawal and isolation to hostile acts of aggression and violence. It includes regression, where a child who has been toilet-trained reverts to wetting the bed, or an older child begins to talk like an infant or toddler. It also includes behaviors such as fighting, throwing food, being the class clown in school, otherwise disrupting class and truancy from school. As the child gets older, these behaviors may include vandalism, shoplifting and other thefts, sexual promiscuity and running away from home.

Of course, the net result of these behaviors is very often more rejection. The child may be suspended or expelled from school. His foster parents may say he has to move to a new foster home. His delinquent behavior may result in placement in a detention home.

More rejection like this means a firmer identity as a worthless person. "See, I told you I was nothing." And this confirmation of his negative self-image will result in an escalation in the anti-social behavior, resulting, of course, in even more rejection.

The child becomes trapped in the self-perpetuating cycle of rejection, negative self-image, and anti-social behavior.

For many children moving from one foster home to another, then another and another, is just a fact of life. Often they don't have a very good understanding of why they are moving. Sometimes it is because of their behavior, but other times it is because of issues in the lives of the foster parents.

Sadly, in some cases children have to move from one foster home to another because of problems on the part of the placement agency. Some foster care agencies are poorly funded and administered. There can be internal agency fighting, inconsistent or constantly changing policies, inadequate staffing, poor training, a lack of an appropriate support system for foster parents, or any number of other problems. As a result, foster parents may not receive the training, supervision, support and relief that they need, and they "burn out." In the end, foster children are the ones who really suffer. They must gather up their few possessions—often times placing them in garbage bags—and move on to the home of a new set of foster parents.

I asked one foster child to give me a history of the various foster homes in which she had lived. Here is what she said:

"My many temporary homes"—Rachel

> Well, my first foster home was when I was around two. I went to Dorothy Jean Neal's. I lived there for like five years, and she was diagnosed with breast cancer, so we went to go live with her son and daughter-in-law in Nashville, Tennessee. We lived there for about a year, but then they couldn't handle my sister and brother. So we moved from there. And then we went to this lady named Ellen in Minerva, and we lived there for about three years. Then we left there to go to Alabama to be adopted. We lived in Alabama for about a month and then our house burned down and they claimed my brother did it.
>
> So we left Alabama and we came back to Canton, and they separated my brother from me and my sister. My sister and I went to this lady named Susan White's house and we lived there about three years. We really did not like it, so after that my sister left and we got split up. And then I left and I went to Ralph and Betty's house, and I lived there about two and one-half months. I left there because they had some kind of charges or something, probably from the other foster children, something happened.

> *Then I left their house and I went to this lady named Mavis Foster. I lived there for about two months.*
>
> *I left her house because I went to the hospital, and she couldn't handle me 'cause she couldn't be home with me enough. I left her house and went to this lady named…I forget her name…I lived there for about a week and went to another home where I stayed about a week and then I went to this foster home, where I've been for about seven months.*

The sense of loss and unfinished business for a child like this must be enormous. She never knew her father. She lost her mother first because of drugs and then through placement. She lost the opportunity to be adopted. She was separated from her brother and sister. And through it all, she has been placed in and removed from eight different foster homes before coming to her most recent home—at the age of 15.

Whether it is because of foster care agency problems or other issues, far too many foster children and youth do not benefit adequately from foster care. The future for these kids is oftentimes very sad and may include homelessness, incarceration, and the need for public assistance.

However, the future for foster children does not have to be so bleak.

The good news is this: carefully selected, well-trained, adequately supervised, and intensively supported foster parents *can* and *do* intervene positively in the lives of neglected and abused children, reversing the cycle of rejection—>negative self image—> anti-social behavior. They do this by accepting children for who they are, helping them see themselves as persons of worth and value, and showing them how to find success in school, work, social and family relationships. The negative cycle can be broken. We have seen it happen many times in the lives of hundreds of different children.

Foster parents *can* and *do* make a difference. In this book, we will hear from foster children about what it takes to meet their needs and to make the foster home experience positive and nurturing.

"My Broken Heart Transfers to a Whole Heart" was drawn by a 16-year-old boy. His birth mom is on the left and his foster mom is on the right. His heart is broken because he is not able to live with his birth mom, but he has hope of healing due to being with a whole family.

Chapter 2
Beginnings

For most children who come into foster care, there is a significant turning point on a specific day at a specific time when people they do not know come and take them away from their parents and place them in a foster home.

Sometimes, these moments are vividly recalled and linger in the memory for a long time, surrounded by great mountains of feelings: hurt, anger, confusion, frustration, disappointment and more.

"Why?"—Leon

Seven years after he was removed from his mother's home, Leon still had questions and feelings about that removal. Here's what he said when I asked him how he felt when they took him away from his parents and placed him in a foster home:

> *I didn't understand anything. They told me this was just temporary, overnight till they could find something, and I didn't understand that. So I just basically went there, they showed me where the TV room was, things like that. They had dinner, they offered dinner, but I didn't want to eat. I was confused and didn't know what was going on. I was mad. I just didn't want to eat at the time. And I went to bed.*

QUESTION: What were you angry about?

> *Well, that they came and took me from my Mom, because I didn't feel, I mean I understood, they explained why a little bit, you know. But I didn't feel it was anybody's right to just barge into my life and tell our family what's right and wrong in our family unit. That's for us to decide. Who can break up our family and tell us what's right for us!* (very animated here) *The way you choose to raise the kids should be up to you. Now I'm glad they did. But questions are still there as far as what I should think now.*

The first day in a new foster home can be really difficult. Think of it! Try to imagine yourself being taken from your home by a social worker (probably you've never seen this person before), removed because your parents—the people supposed to nurture and protect you—had abused you or failed to meet your needs. Or perhaps that had happened long ago, and now you are being removed from one foster home to go to another.

All sorts of thoughts and questions are running through your head. "What are these new people like? How will they treat me? Will they really care about me, or are they in it for the money? Will I ever see my mom and dad or my brother and sister again? What will happen to them? What about my friends in my old neighborhood? Will they know what happened to me? Will they care? Will they think I'm a bad person because I was placed in a foster home? What will the new school be like? Will I be able to make new friends, or will they turn away from me because I'm a foster child?"

How can foster parents ease the transition to their home, and help to make the first day of placement a positive, reassuring experience for foster children?

Overwhelmingly, foster children want to know that they are wanted by the new family. They want to know that they are not a burden, but rather that the family is pleased to have them there.

"They were happy when I came"—Margaret

Margaret was a teenage mother when she came to live with the Roth family. She had lived in another foster home and that had not worked out very well. But she was fortunate in that she knew the Roths because of having gone there on respite. She felt comfortable with them.

The Roths had six children of their own when Margaret came to live with them:

> *Yeah, they were all really excited and happy when I came. They all seemed real bubbly. I had met them once before I went to live with them, when I lived with the Ratheon family. I had come down to my Mom's for Christmas, and my Mom wasn't there and I got sick. I was nursing my baby, and I had to go to the neighbor's to go to the hospital because I was really badly infected. And my Mom was out drinking, I think, and I called Terri [caseworker], I believe, and Terri came and got me and she took me to the Roths to spend the night. So I had met them once before and they seemed really, really nice.*
>
> *But when I was placed with them, they were just like, just real bubbly, full of life people. They showed me around, helped set up my room, and went over the rules and the phone limitations, and as far as people coming over…And what they expected, like chore-wise. They have a chore list that they divide among all the kids, different weeks. And we just went over all that stuff and they were really, really nice people.*

Margaret appreciated the Roths for the way in which they welcomed her into their home. They seemed happy to have her there, went out of their way to make her comfortable, and made sure that she understood their expectations of her. It was a good beginning.

"Not just a foster kid"—Amy

Amy had lived in several foster homes before she came to the Revianos. At that time, she was 16 years old and had been separated from her parents for five years. Here she recounts her first day in the new foster home:

> *My first day? Well, I really remember… Your first impression, when you come through the door, is how you know the rest of your time will be. You can always tell. When I walked through the door, she smiled at me and I knew, you know, everything was going to be OK.*
>
> *And I was really scared and I didn't know what to think, because I had just got taken out of one [foster] home and put into another. I had all these thoughts going through my mind. And to me she understood. And I was thinking to myself, you know…so scared. We talked and stuff and I told her how I felt, and it was like, she really understood. Because you can't, I mean, for some people, you can't say, 'I know how you feel,' if you've never gone through that before. But it always helps when somebody talks to you. And…even if they don't know how you feel, it's good to have a hug once in a while and for them to say, you know, 'It's going to be OK.'*
>
> *'Cause I remember this was the only foster home where that had happened and I knew my experience was going to be great because this family understood me and helped me feel comfortable.*
>
> *It wasn't like 'Oh, no! Here comes another child.' It was like, 'I'm taking care of another child. I'm helping somebody out. Making a difference, you know, in her life. She is not just living here and I'm givin' her three meals a day, sending her to school. It's not that way.'*

> *In the other foster home I was at, the foster mother had two other children who didn't really like me and we never got along. It didn't really matter to my foster mother that they didn't like me. It was like I would do something wrong and she would yell at me. And then they would do the same thing and nothing happened. It looked like the birth children thought, 'You're just a foster kid. You're not the same. Since she's my mom, not yours, that makes the whole situation different.' And it was really hard.*
>
> *When somebody's really interested in you, they'll ask you questions and you know how they really care about you. They will tell you the things that bother them and what they want. They don't yell at you. It's like, you know, these things are what I want to talk about and how we can change it. In the other home, it was like my foster mom wouldn't mention things that bothered her, and then when a big old blowup came, she was like, 'You did this, this and this, and I don't like that.' And usually, you need to talk about those things and not just blow up at somebody like that, because they don't know, they don't understand. But you can always tell when somebody does not accept you. I mean, it can be for many reasons.*

When Amy came to her new home, she sensed that the foster parent was different from a previous foster parent—open and accepting of her, as she was. She seemed to feel confident that the foster parent understood her feelings, even if the foster parent had never been in a similar situation herself.

Due to having lived with abuse and therefore needing to know how people are going to react to them and treat them, foster children often possess a heightened sense of awareness of the feelings of those around them. They have trained themselves to pick up cues in the body language, mannerisms and statements of people, cues that tell them what to expect. Trying to put on a front and pretend to be caring when we don't feel caring rarely works with foster children.

Of course, we all can be affected by stress. This turmoil in our lives can impact the cues that we give off. We may have had some distressing news about one of our parents or perhaps our own children have been particularly difficult. In such a case, the new foster child in our home may "read" us wrong, thinking that perhaps the frown may mean that we don't like them. If you have had a difficult day, it will be important to "bracket" these problems, setting them aside temporarily, so that when the foster child comes to your home, you can be 100 percent there for the child. This is not just putting on a front. Rather, it is providing recognition that this foster child is a very important person, deserving of a welcome to our home. First impressions do mean a lot.

"They talked to me"—Erin

Erin had also lived in other foster homes. She had lived in one home, the Watsons, for four years before coming to the placement described in this account. The Watsons were having marital problems, however, and she experienced their home as being cold and unresponsive to her. Here, she compares her experiences in the two different homes:

> *The foster family I was with before, I really didn't connect with because they had built up this wall, you know. It seemed like they didn't want to get too close to foster kids, because they knew these kids would leave one day. But there's also a point where foster parents need to get to know the kids and make them feel more comfortable. I never felt comfortable with that family. However, living with that family helped me realize what was important to me and what wasn't.*
>
> *At first, I was scared when I had to move from that family, because I did not know how the next family would relate to me. But when I came to live with Mr. and Mrs. Stanley, I felt like they cared. It was like, 'We have another foster kid. We want to make it work.' They talked to me and listened to me. We talked about a lot of things. And there were moments, you know, when I didn't know what was going to happen, but then, just like any normal family, we worked things out.*

Erin felt that problems were never really worked through in

her former foster family. Perhaps because of the marital problems in the family, Erin felt that she did not really form relationships with the foster parents. She was there and they were there, but they never really met each other in a deep and personal way. How sad for Erin, but for the foster family too, who missed the opportunity to find joy in the richness and depth of another human being.

> when I first
> Met You
> I was scard
> To Tell you
> That I love you

"WHEN I FIRST MET YOU" was written by a 6-year-old boy who was recalling his early mixed feelings of fear and love for his new adoptive mother.

Chapter 3
The Hunger for Family

Foster children want to belong to a family. Some will never again live with their birth families and some will not be adopted. Still, they want to belong to a family. They want to know that someone is committed to them, cares deeply about them, and accepts them for who they are. They want to be needed by their families and to be significant and important to these people. They want to know that they matter to someone.

Foster children are sometimes hyper-vigilant toward any sign that they are being treated differently than other children living in the same home. They are acutely aware of the unfairness of their situation to begin with—being away from their own families while other children can be with their birth parents. Any indication that the foster family is showing favoritism for their birth children, giving them gifts or privileges that the foster children do not get, will activate feelings of hurt and alienation for the foster children.

When I interviewed Angela, who had lived in many foster homes, the interview did not go well. Perhaps because of the hurt that she had experienced throughout her life in so many different ways, Angela seemed to have disconnected her feelings from her experiences. It was hard for her to talk about feelings other than anger, even though I could see there was a lot of hurt buried deep within. In this portion of the interview, I had asked Angela if there were any reasons for her high level of anger toward one of her foster families:

> ANGELA: *Oh yeah. There were a lot of reasons. She had two sons and like, everything would be just fine with them, but me and my sister Teresa were just always starting trouble. Like, even if their sons did something wrong, me and Teresa were accused of causing it.*
>
> QUESTION: So you were always blamed?
> ANGELA: *Yeah. She would be like, 'We can't all go out and do something, because we have to run you and your sister everywhere. It's ruining our family.' So, it was just really awful. I didn't like her.*
>
> QUESTION: How did it make you feel?
> ANGELA: *It made me really mad.*
>
> QUESTION: Usually anger is preceded by hurt. Perhaps you were really hurt by how the foster mother related to you?
> ANGELA: *Yeah. 'Cause like, she was OK for the first couple months, and then she just switched automatically. It wasn't like a subtle change, it was really quick.*

Angela never had the experience of being wanted by this family. She was always an outsider, a burden and inconvenience for them. Even for those children who will someday return to live with their parents or be adopted, the need to belong to this temporary family is very strong.

In the following accounts, Marie, Rosalynn, Andrew and Lance speak of their longing to belong to a family and the ways in which their foster parents have incorporated them into their families.

"I JUST WANTED TO BE A PART OF THEIR FAMILY"—MARIE

In this account, Marie contrasts living with two different foster families. In the first paragraph, she speaks of a foster family situation that did not work out for her because her need to belong to the family was not being satisfied. With the Schmidts, however, she had a happier experience:

> *[One day] you know it just kinda hit me like a brick wall. From that moment on I realized that I would never really be part of their family. And I really wanted to be. I thought it was my fault that it fell out at their family because I just wanted to be part of their family. When I realized I really wasn't ever gonna be, I started acting out a lot. Although they were really good people, and they were really nice, I didn't feel comfortable in their home.*
>
> *But when I lived with the Schmidts, you know, they didn't get upset with me when I did things that were wrong. They would say, 'Yeah, Marie, you screwed up. Let's deal with it and go on.' You know, they never judged me for being a bad kid or anything like that. That was like the best foster home I was in…I love Mr. and Mrs. Schmidt, they're like family, you know, and that means a lot to me.*
>
> *They worked with me on things, they talked to me, and they let me be my own person. You know, they didn't try to control what I did and everything, like my boyfriend who I met when I was in their home. He is my husband now. He's my soul mate. When I lived with the Schmidts, they let my boyfriend come over often, and he would have dinner with us and everything. They make you feel like family, you know. And they were all real affectionate.*

But when I lived with another foster family, they were so worried about me hugging them, there was no emotional connection there. I couldn't hug them, they didn't feel comfortable with that, you know. There was no emotional contact or anything like that.

And with the Schmidts, we would go to church on Sundays and I felt accepted and cared for by the people at church. There was a lot of emotional connection with others in the church.

It wasn't uncomfortable for me to receive and give hugs when I lived in the Schmidt home. Everything felt really natural there. I think that's probably what it was. There was stability and emotional connection there, and they were able to be affectionate and not feel uncomfortable with a foster child in the house.

And they would talk to me a lot, when I would screw up, like with school and stuff. They'd sit down with me and talk to me about my consequences. Or like if they heard something about me, instead of automatically jumping the gun…they would sit down and ask me, 'Well, look, Marie, we heard this, and we want to know what the situation is.' And they just kept the lines of communication open, you know, they didn't close me off. They listened to what I had to say, and they cared about what I had to say and how I felt that day. If I was in a bad mood or whatever, they wanted to know why, what happened and everything. They were just really open and really supportive with me, and I think that's probably what makes the Schmidts a good foster home… for me, anyways. I mean, some people might be uncomfortable with them, but I wasn't.

Matching a child with foster parents is an extremely important part of what a children's agency does. As Marie said at the end, some children might be uncomfortable with the open expression of love and affection in the Schmidt's home, but, for her, it was a very effective way of conveying acceptance.

Sometimes we get a good match, and sometimes we aren't as successful. However, to the extent that foster parents can remain genuine, they should adapt their relational style to the needs of the child in their home. Flexibility can be very helpful.

"I didn't know what to call them"—Rosalynn

Foster children frequently don't know how to define the relationship between themselves and their foster parents. "What should I call these people? Mr. and Mrs.? Aunt and Uncle? Bob and Mary? Mom and Dad? What am I to them and what should they be to me?"

The confusion is compounded because of loyalties to birth parents. "How do I relate to the people who gave me birth and now aren't able to care for me? What am I to them and what should they be to me?"

We can short-circuit the confusion by telling the foster child to call us this or that. It's usually better, however, to allow the foster child to struggle with the question and come to his or her own resolution, one that is comfortable and right for him or her. Rosalynn struggled with these questions.

> When I moved in, like I knew I was living there now but it still didn't quite register. I felt like really weird. I didn't know what to call the Wests. I didn't know if I should call them Mr. and Mrs. West, Mom and Dad, or Jan and Dick; so I just said like 'Hey.' I was really nervous about it, I don't know. I wouldn't pick up the phone even though I knew I could, I was allowed. Just like things you would do in your own home, I was kind of afraid to do. It was kind of weird. It took me about a month to get over all of that.
>
> I think that the Wests helped me a lot in the sense that they always made sure that I knew that their home was my home. They didn't treat me any differently, as if I didn't really live there. But I think a lot of it had to just come to me. I had to get used to everything and kind of had to settle myself in to know everybody until I felt comfortable living that way. I had to feel comfortable calling them Mom and Dad. Now it just seems like second nature.
>
> I was kind of afraid to ask about what to call them. The first time I ever called them 'Mom and Dad,' I felt kind of funny. They kind of gave me a look like 'Now you're opening up.' After

a while though, it got easier. They didn't care what I called them. I called them whatever I felt comfortable with. So that helped a lot, really.

As Rosalyn matured and became more comfortable in her foster home, she became more comfortable with calling her foster parents "Mom and Dad West."

One foster parent that I knew told children who came into her home that they could call her by a name that was different than that used for their birth mothers. For example, if they called their birth mothers "Mommy," they could call the foster mother "Mom" or "Mother." This helped the child to distinguish between the two mother figures in his or her own mind.

"They treated me like one of their own"—Andrew

Andrew stayed with the same foster family during six years of care. He developed a good relationship with his foster family. At the same time, he maintained connections with his birth mother who remained involved and visited frequently.

He talks about the foster parents as his "people," and still visits them. There is a very strong bond between Andrew and the foster family. He is now serving in the Navy, but still remains connected to his foster family.

> *Most of my life I have been shifted around from place to place. My dad and my mom, they were divorced when I was three or four years old, something like that. Since then, I had never been in a mother and father environment. My dad, he's been married I don't know how many times. He moved from here to there.*
>
> *But this [the foster home] is just a stable environment, a family environment. There's two parents, plus the uncles and all that. They took me on from the beginning, just took me in and all that.*
>
> *[After I came here] I didn't have to worry about moving around and all that. I could always depend on my people.*

> They [the foster parents] treated me like I was one of their own sons. That's the way it has always been. Not a bit of difference, just like their birth sons.
>
> They were constantly staying on me with the schooling. Education has always been important. I've always liked sports but wasn't really as active before I went there.
>
> Church was also an important factor for me. We went to church together every Sunday. My foster mom said that church comes before other things. The Lord is the one who gave you the talent and the strength to do everything, so that's always first.
>
> All my breaks from the military, I'm coming home here, phone calls, letters, all that. Like she told me, just 'cause I'm 18 and leaving, it's not the end.
>
> She's always basically told me that. She said I'm always welcome. It's always my home and I'm always welcome.

Perhaps the highest compliment a foster child can pay his foster parents is this statement, "They treated me like one of their own."

"She cares"—Lance

Lance had lived in several different foster homes before going to live with the Milanos. He was 17 at the time, but he still wanted to know that someone really cared about him.

> When I was working at Burger King one night, I noticed more that she was concerned. One night I was working past the time I was supposed to get off. After I was about an hour late, she sent her husband to come and get me…when we got home, she said she was really worried. And you could tell that she was genuinely worried and scared…didn't know where I was, didn't know what had happened, if I had gotten beaten up or mugged or whatever. I felt bad about it, that I had made her worry or something. But about a day later, I realized that her concern made me feel good because it showed that she cares.
>
> So I guess this has been the best place I've been. I don't worry about nothing. We're real relaxed.

How true it is that when we care about someone, when we are deeply involved with someone, we experience anxiety when their whereabouts are unknown or they have been gone longer than we expect. It is quite appropriate, when the child returns safe and sound, to let him or her know that we were concerned. Often an appropriate, calm expression of concern over the safety of the child will be more effective than any disciplinary action. She or he will be more likely to respond to genuine caring by informing the foster family the next time there is an unexpected change of schedule.

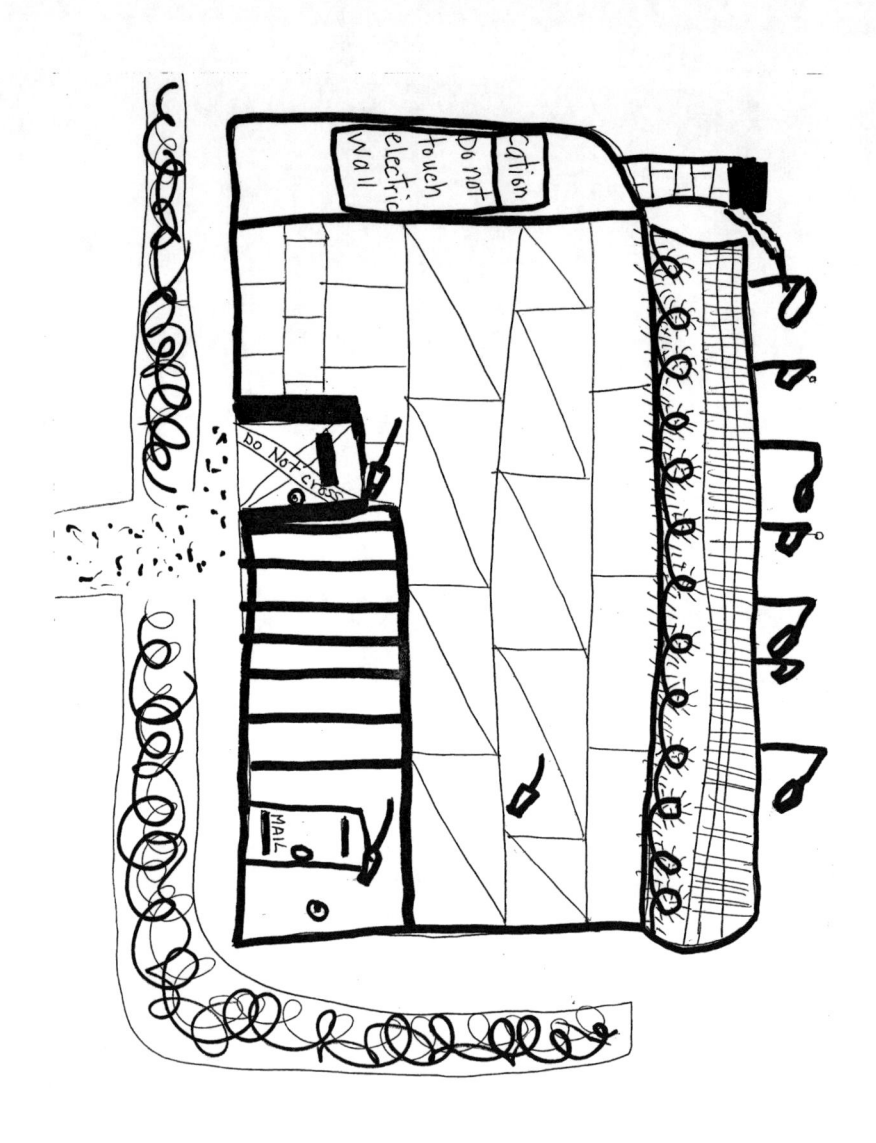

"WALL OF PROTECTION" was drawn by an 11-year-old boy who was asked to show the wall he put up against others due to several moves in foster care. He said that he would only allow contact from the world to his heart through the small door or mail slot.

Chapter 4
Why Do They Do That?

We are often bewildered by the foster children who come into our lives. We try to give them love and compassion. We suffer with them through their questions about their parents, their physical illnesses, their problems in school and with peers. We are sometimes up late talking with them about their concerns and up early the next morning to take them to an activity.

After all this, we often encounter verbal abuse, angry words that don't seem to be deserved, words that come from some well deep within the child that we cannot access.

"I understood in a way, but it still hurt"—Foster Dad

> *I will never forget the Thanksgiving Day we spent with our foster child. My wife had prepared a wonderful dinner, and we had all enjoyed it.*
>
> *Still, late in the afternoon, I found our foster child on the front porch, staring wistfully out across the street. I knew he was thinking, 'I wish I could be with my Mom today. I wish I could have had this time with her today.'*
>
> *I could understand his deep down desire to be at home. It seemed perfectly reasonable, a homesickness that I would have felt if I had been in his shoes. But, I couldn't help my own feelings. After all we had done and given to him, it still hurt that he wanted to be somewhere other than with us.*

Why do foster children act the way they do? Why do they have so much difficulty accepting and returning love? Why do they so often give back anger instead?

"Betty was afraid of a better world"—Susan

During foster care, Susan changed from a very withdrawn and isolated teenager, deeply involved in depression, to a bright and outgoing young lady who is now attending college, studying journalism. Here, she tells us about a younger child who lived in the foster home with her, a child who could not accept the love of her foster parents because accepting that love created overwhelming fear in her.

> *It's hard to let someone new come into your house. And it's hard to go into the home of someone new. Foster parents should just try to understand that the kids, where they come from, it's often times not a good place and so they may be hard to deal with. Betty, for example, would have temper tantrums all the time.*
>
> *But it's not the foster parents themselves that is the hardest thing for kids. I would say that if anything, the biggest problem with kids when they come from abused or bad situations, is that they're afraid of the better world.*
>
> *You're afraid that there is something better. It's like you try*

to keep it from yourself. You try to stay where you feel safe. That's what you know, even if what you know is bad.

Alice [foster mother] tried, I tried, and Heather [birth daughter of the foster family] tried to show Betty that it wasn't going to be bad like other places. We would play games with Betty, we would read her stories, and I think she was the same as me. She wasn't used to that. And I think that whenever something like that happens, I think usually you think 'What do they want back for it?' Usually that was the way it was.

Often times in abuse situations if you do this, if you get something good, it means something bad is going to come with it.

I don't know if she was expecting that or not. But that's how a lot of times it is, and I think that a lot of good things happened, and so even though it scared Betty when it would happen, I think she would throw temper tantrums to try to break it up. I mean to break the bond that might be created. Something good will happen again, then she would think something bad would happen. I think it was a matter of who could persevere longer.

Because that is where she is comfortable. You become what you know because that is what you're comfortable with. Even if it is abuse that you know, that is what you're comfortable with.

I'll use myself as an example, it was hard because the foster parents were nice, but the nicer it got, the worse the memories got. Because, when you feel safer, the memories start to surface. Then you either throw a tantrum and try to put yourself back in the safety net where you can block everything out, or you try to beat the wall down and keep going.

When I interviewed Susan, I was so affected by her honesty and her revelation of herself, and the stress that foster children feel, that I choked back tears. How infinitely sad that a child must view life in terms of a quid pro quo, that if I accept something good, something bad will happen to me! And how courageous and persevering foster parents must be, when confronted by this world view!

To help the child see the world in different terms, to help them accept love that does not require unpleasant trades, to help them know that love is their right as human beings—this is the challenge that confronts many foster parents.

"What else can I do to get them to kick me out?"
—Heather

Heather had been abandoned by her parents. She lived in several group homes and was sometimes hospitalized for emotional difficulties. All the group homes eventually gave up on her because of her running away, sexual promiscuity and drug-oriented behavior. When she went to live with the Hansons, however, she found some people who were more stubborn than she was, and who would not give up on her.

Heather used many different behavior problems to try to get the family to fulfill her personal life definition, which was that no one could ever live with her. In her case, their love was stronger than her self-confusion:

> *Kate [foster mother] said she just kept me here because she said I was part of the family and that just throwing me out was not going to handle it. She said the only way anybody is going to learn is to sit down and talk to them about it. She just said that if we can't work it out here, then we'll get some help for it. She always said her and I could work anything out. I mean I'd cuss her out and call her everything, but we'd just sit down and talk about it and stuff.*
>
> *Well, I think it is mainly because Kate tries so hard to help me and stuff. I mean like when I saw my mom in October. That did not go well at all. Kate is always there to help me and comfort me and she just tells me 'Everything will be okay, I'm your mom now.' When she says that, I feel better. I mean it doesn't matter if I call someone in my family and they could just hurt me as bad as they want to, Kate would be there to pick me up. So I really like her for that. She always tells me when I start to feel like I don't belong here, then she always helps me to remember that I do fit in here, I do belong here. And Jim, he just puts humor into everything. Something really bad can happen and he finds something funny about it.*

When I would get into trouble and do stupid things, they would stick with me, and a lot of times when I would do stupid stuff, people would just say, 'Get her out! We don't want her here.' I mean like Kate told me, she goes, 'If I stick by, no matter what you do, and I help you to get over it, to find something better to do, then it's not going to hurt you or anybody else. Then you're going to be okay.' She goes, 'If people just give up on you all the time, you're not going to get anywhere. You're just going to think you're a failure.' So every time I got in trouble at school or something like that, I would just come home and she would be like, 'Okay, we need to talk.' I mean I used to do things to try and get her to kick me out of here.

Why? I don't know. I have no idea why. But she wouldn't do it. She kept telling me, 'I'm not going to kick you out no matter what you do, because I know that's what you want me to do. You're stuck here and you're stuck with me and my family.' And then I'd be like, you know, I don't care if I'm stuck here with you and your family.

Then I would try to figure out another way. 'Okay, let's see what else I can do to get them to kick me out.'

Let's see. What have I done? Well, she told me that I wasn't permitted to do drugs or drink here and no drugs were allowed into this house, if I did I was out of here. So that gets into my head, 'Go buy a dime. You'll get yourself kicked out.'

So I went out and bought a 'dime,' which is like $10 worth of marijuana, in case you didn't know. So I brought it here and kept it hid and later on I was like, 'Do you want to go and get my marijuana for me?' She was like, 'Sure,' and she went and flushed it down the toilet. Didn't kick me out or anything.

I was like, 'This isn't fair. You told me that if I brought drugs into the house, you were going to kick me out.' She goes, 'That's why you brought it in.' She was like, 'I'm not going to kick you out.' Then after a while I just gave up. She told me that she wasn't kicking me out because 'You want kicked out too bad. You're stuck.' I would just think 'Okay. If I'm stuck, I'm stuck.'

When I first moved in I didn't trust anybody. It was, like, if you raise your hand towards me, and you were just waving *goodbye, I'd just jump. I mean, it scared me. It still does some to this day. If somebody comes up real quick to give me a hug, it scares me, and I jump back. It's like when I first moved in, nobody touched me. I hated to be touched, especially around my neck and my shoulders. So after a while we got over that. Kate would just catch me off guard and would give me a hug. And even though I squirmed to get away, it wouldn't work. She told me she was going to break me of the habit.*

Foster parents will be tested by the foster children in their homes. They will probably be tested many times, in many different ways. After a while, after you have lived with the child for a time and passed some tests, the testing may subside for a time. Please don't think that your testing and trials with this child are over and in the past. Like the rest of us, during times of stress, the child will revert to old ways of thinking and relating, and our love and our patience will be challenged again. And once more you must not give up.

At the height of World War II, Winston Churchill spoke to a group. His speech consisted of six words: "Never…never…never…never…give up." This should be the motto of all foster parents, and parents too.

"THEY RESPECT ME"—JEREMY

Jeremy has lived in 15 different foster homes since he was four years old. He reported that, in the beginning, he tried to create as many behavior problems as possible because he believed that if his behavior were unmanageable, the system would let him go back home. But that didn't happen, and it seemed that eventually acting bad became a habit, out of his control.

Among other things, Jeremy had a terrible temper that was usually well-hidden. When it was seen, however, it was like the eruption of Mount Vesuvius. Out would come the most terrible comments, threats and insults. That's what happened one day with his foster mother, Dorothy. What she and her husband did after this event, however, has made a lasting impact on Jeremy.

> *I had a problem not too long ago. Probably about two months ago. Charlie [another foster child] had gotten up in my face, and I shoved him and started punching him. Dorothy sent him to his room. And she told me that I was out of line. I started arguing with her about it. I had had a friend stay over that night. She told my friend that it was time to go, get his stuff, she was gonna take him home.*
>
> *Then I said, 'Well, I'm leaving too.' I started cussin', swearin' and arguin'. I went in the living room and threw my shoes. My friend had never, ever seen me like this before. I was yellin' at my foster mom. And he grabbed me by my shoulder, when I was talkin' to my mom, and I turned around and grabbed him and slammed him onto the couch. I was so far out of control, I guess I hit him a couple of times, I didn't even know I did it. And, uh, I left. I guess I ran away. I called Pathway and they took me to the group home for a couple days. And when I settled down, we had a meeting, talked about it or whatever.*
>
> *In the meeting, we talked about what we were going to do. Like ways to overcome situations like that. We talked about what had happened.*
>
> *I went back to counseling and to an anger management class. And still to this day we're working on it; still healing, I guess.*
>
> *I mean, I really, really hurt Dorothy emotionally, cut her down emotionally. Something like that, it's not going to heal overnight. It's like you had a son that you were really close to, and he got shot, died. The next day, you're not gonna be out bowling or something like that. So we're still working on it.*

So far in these interviews several children have talked about the need to work through problems. Working through problems is a skill that good families practice on a regular basis. We cannot just walk away after a problem, pretend that it is over and done, and go on as if nothing happened. We must sit down together and process the problem, look at what caused it, how we reacted and what we could do differently in the future.

When we refuse to work through problems, we are in a sense stockpiling them as ammunition for future conflicts. In those conflicts, we can bring up these unresolved issues: "You did this and this and this" or "You always do this."

Working through problems is part of never giving up, being committed to one another.

"The hardest thing was the memories coming back" —Samantha

Children do not forget the abuse and neglect that they have experienced. It's a part of their lives, a part of who they have become. They will need to spend many different periods of time going back, consciously and unconsciously, to the experiences, reworking them, coming to understanding and acceptance of these experiences.

When children are in this process of coming to terms with their life experiences, we will sometimes see them doing strange things, things we don't understand. Sometimes, this will involve regressing to old patterns of behavior, old ways of doing things which, because of their familiarity, bring comfort and reassurance.

In these times, sometimes all foster parents can do is stand nearby, ready to offer hope and help.

> *The memories coming back was probably the hardest for me. I suppose it was the worst. When the memories first started coming back, they seemed real to me. That is another reason I am glad I was at Rick and Donna's [foster parents]. It's often times when you have the memories that it's hard to realize that [they're not real] instead of thinking that you are back there.*
>
> *The feelings are so strong. That is the hardest thing. When you have those feelings if someone says something that is good to you, you're at your most vulnerable point. I think I was. Like, whenever I would have my memory, I would go upstairs and take a bath and cry. Donna would knock on the door and say, 'Samantha, are you okay?'*
>
> *I'd say, 'Yeah. Just let me be. Don't come in.' Or, I might have said, 'Yes, just go away.' I was putting up that wall so I wouldn't have to worry about anybody else.*

> *Now, it's kind of different because I can remember those things and it still hurts, but it doesn't seem so real any more. I think a lot of kids when they first come from abuse, it is real. That is what they know—that's their life.*

Unfortunately, abuse is one of the life experiences of too many children. It has a strong influence on the person they will eventually become. Some will blame their abuser for "ruining" their lives, while others can and do overcome the effects of abuse and go on to live happy and productive lives. There may be scars, external and/or internal, resulting from the abuse, but life can be beautiful and fulfilling in spite of the scars.

The same circumstances that destroy one person will make another stronger. It must be something within the individual that makes the difference. That something has to come from somewhere (from God, I believe) and can be used constructively by individuals who make the choice to do so.

I believe that staff and foster parents can be tools in the hands of the Heavenly Father—tools for instilling this special something that allows a child to overcome. We must, however, be very patient and not barge into a child's life with our advice or admonitions. However, we can stand, knocking on the door, as this foster mom did, ready to listen and support the child when he or she is ready.

"I KNOW THEY DIDN'T REALLY LIKE ME"—CHARLES

As I stated previously, if you are a foster parent, you are constantly being tested, in little ways and in big ways. After all, as you are telling this child that you care about him, he is remembering the abuse that he received from his own parents, who were supposed to care about him. And he is also recalling the other foster families with whom he has lived, who also said they cared about him. Your foster child will ask himself, "How can I believe them this time?"

And the only way he can believe that you care is to test that caring. And test it again…and again…and again.

Will you pass the test? How sad that the family Charles is talking about here did not pass. It is sad for him, because he will look back on yet another experience of people who abandoned him. But it is sad for the foster family too, who must experience the wrenching sense of failure at the task of really loving this child.

> *During the first few weeks that my brother and I lived in their foster home, I stayed in my room a lot. 'Cause I didn't know what I was gonna do, if I was gonna make friends or not. It was like somethin' new to me. I was kinda shy then, but after about a month passed by, I started getting along with everyone.*
>
> *I probably stayed in that home about half a year. But then the parents, they went on vacation, and they didn't know if they were allowed taking us or not, and the court finally moved us.*
>
> *For moving from home to home, at first, I wasn't so used to it. I didn't like it a whole lot. But now that I'm used to it, it doesn't really bother me.*
>
> *I mean I'm used to it, but in another way I'm not because I would actually like to stay at one home instead of moving from place to place.*
>
> *[The former foster parents] would probably say that I was a little thief and they didn't actually like me. And then there were times that they'd say they cared about me. But I didn't really believe it a whole lot. In some ways, I know they didn't really like me.*
>
> *I mean, they probably cared about me somewhat when I first got there. But with everything that had gone on, I started thinking that they're probably not gonna care about me much longer. 'Cause after a while, I'd go out of my room [when I was grounded] and my foster mother wouldn't care. I'd go outside, run around with my friends, she wouldn't care. I'd leave their property, she wouldn't care.*
>
> *She should have told me if I was grounded to my room, to go back to my room. That's what my new foster parent does. If I'm grounded, she'll sit me on the couch. And if I move off that couch, if I go upstairs to play, she'll tell me to come downstairs and sit on the couch. That's why I like her, 'cause she actually sticks with things that she says.*

> *I can actually tell that she loves me, because at night we actually talk and anytime I get into trouble, they'll tell me what I did wrong and why I shouldn't do it again.*

A child should never have to get used to moving from foster home to foster home. A child should never have to wonder if the mistake he made today will mean that he must go to a new home tomorrow. A child should never have to ask herself if she will be able to live in this home this coming Christmas.

They do, however. And because human beings dislike ambiguity, if a child feels that he might have to move, he may do things to force the move. At least then he will be in control of the moving, rather than leaving it up to other people to make a decision about where he will sleep tonight.

People who want to be foster parents must be able to communicate with a child, with their actions as well as their words, that they like the child. Sometimes, as Charles says, they will do this by enforcing the discipline that they have imposed.

"Pushing the Hurt Away" was drawn by a 10-year-old boy.

Chapter 5
Living Through the Problems

There is a joy to be found in foster parenting that cannot come in any other way. However, the joy belongs only to the foster parents who won't give up, who won't be worn down by the child's efforts to make them reject him or her. The joy belongs to the foster parents who are committed to seeing this child through good times and bad, through name-calling, destruction of property, angry outbursts, running away, lying, stealing or countless other behaviors. Only when you've gone through the worst that the child has to offer without rejecting and turning the child away, only then will the child open up and let your love flow in.

Sadly, foster parents often deprive themselves of this joy because they give up too easily. To reach the joy, foster parents must go through great sadness, because the children with whom they live have experienced great sadness. To live with these children is to expose oneself to knowing and feeling the great trauma and hurt that they have experienced in their lives.

Sometimes, when these children act out their problems and test our protestations of love for them, we feel as if something in us has died.

And the feeling is right. Something has died—the naïve belief that we can help these children grow out of their hurt without experiencing that hurt with them.

We must go through the hurt, living through the problem, in order to see the child bloom like a delicate, precious flower.

If we give up at the time of the hurt, we will deprive ourselves of the joy that comes on the other side.

"One of the Worst Times"—Theresa

Theresa has lived in the same foster home for seven years. In this interview, she recalled a time in which she violated the trust of her foster mother. In so doing, she was regressing to an earlier time in her life in which females did what the males in their lives told them to do, regardless of their own knowledge of right and wrong.

> *One of the worst times was when I kinda played in an act with these boys that stayed at our house. They wanted to steal our foster parent's car, and I kinda had a role in that. I had to page them and let them know that my foster mother was sleeping, that everything was cool. I felt really bad, like paranoid. That was rough.*
>
> *It was terrible. All I did was go around and cry. Every night I prayed to the Lord that everybody would forgive me and I thought that the Lord would never forgive me. And it was really awkward.*
>
> *One of the boys had told his father about it, and his father reported it to the caseworker. Finally, the truth had to come out either way, and so I just brought it up. I confessed. My foster mother cried. She felt torn. She was very emotionally dispirited*

and upset.

After that she had a rough time trusting me. And now I feel like I can't lie to her at all, I can't do anything that's untrustworthy or dishonest, anything like that. I'm always faithful towards her.

When I saw that she was so torn by what I had done, I felt guilty and upset because she was upset and because I had done something like that to her and…upset at the boys, for getting me involved in something like that. And upset at myself too, for allowing it.

And I was scared that I wouldn't be able to live in that home anymore, because I had violated her so badly. That was really scary.

We got through it by every night talking about it and expressing how we felt and getting to know what our standards would become…and understanding and trusting each other. Building the trust in the relationship, like a mother and daughter.

You have to communicate. You've got to be able to talk about stuff like that, you can't just hide it. 'Cause if you hide it, it's going to become a big ball of fire and you're going to end up committing suicide because of guilt, or you're going to end up being delinquent or criminal or take it out on everybody else.

In situations like this, the foster parents must try to understand where the kids are coming from. Some of them won't listen and try to understand. Maybe they've never been in that type of situation before. Or perhaps they have been in a similar situation, and they know what it's like, but they don't feel like listening to it over and over again. Perhaps they don't feel like they want to bring back the memories of similar things in their own lives. They try to get beyond the memories and stuff by not talking about things.

There are few guarantees in life, but there is one thing we can count on: when we live with other people, including foster children, there will be problems. There will be times when the testing becomes so great that we don't think we can continue in the relationship. When you reach that time, I encourage you to take a deep breath, sit back, and think about what life might be like for this child if you give up on him or her. Perhaps then you need to talk to your caseworker, or someone else that might be objective about your needs and those of the child, about what you can do to change the situation.

"We talk about it and get through it"—Erin

Children know that problems don't just go away without talking about them. The existence of an unresolved problem, conflict, or disagreement creates anxiety and tension for the foster child. There is a yearning for resolution, for return to a status where this conflict does not interfere with the relationship. Erin contrasted the two foster homes in which she has lived for the ways in which they handled conflict:

> *The other foster family I had lived with, their solution to conflict was just to brush it underneath the rug, and not talk about it. And sometimes that made things...harder you know. And they would just forget about it, but then maybe another situation similar to that would arise. It would be full-blown, even if it would be over something small. To them it was this huge, big old thing. With every kid, they come with a whole bag-load of problems that can make things much harder.*
>
> *In this foster home, me and my foster mom may be arguing and stuff and, you know, everything will be fine, and then like the next day, there'll be like that tension there, and you just can't seem to get along without solving that problem. So we'll sit down and talk about it.*
>
> *But at the other place where I was at, it was just like, 'We don't care. You work it out on your own, and whatever happens, happens.' But here, you know, it's different. We talk about it and get through it, you know. And it's not like, 'Forget it.'*
>
> *And...the differences here: I remember an argument me and her [birth] daughter had and she said she wasn't going to choose between us two 'cause she wanted to be equal about it and I really liked that. Because it wasn't like... she wasn't choosing sides*

or anything. She wanted us to work it out. She was like, 'You girls take care of it; I'm not choosing sides. I can't choose between my daughter and a foster child.' You know, and to me that was really good, because she respected us to the point where we could make our own decisions and it wasn't like, 'I'm on her side, because she's my daughter.' It just doesn't work that way. Even now, she doesn't, you know, it's like me and her daughter are sisters, I mean, well in a way we are, since I live here and everything. She really makes things very equal.

Knowing when to talk about a problem is as important as knowing that you must talk about it. Sometimes, after a problem, we need a little space, a little cooling off period. Don't try to talk to the child about a problem when either your temper or the child's is boiling over. And don't force the child to talk about the problem when he or she is not ready. Let them know that you are there to talk when they are ready.

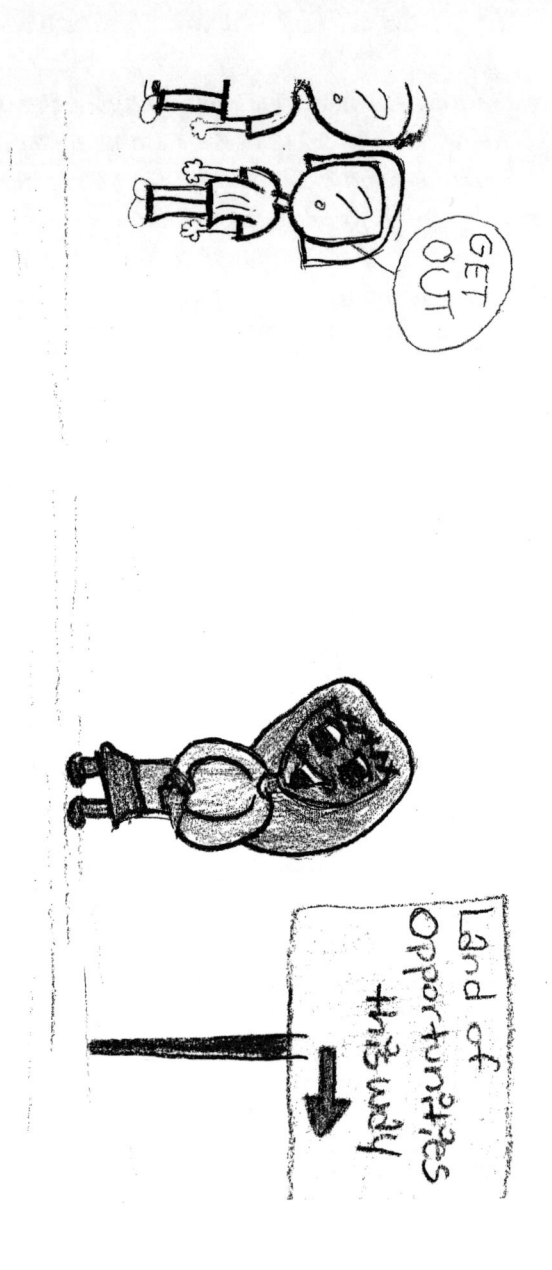

"LAND OF OPPORTUNITIES" was drawn by an 11-year-old girl. Her birth parents are on the left. She plans to go to college because of the support of her adoptive family.

Chapter 6
Moving On With Life

Foster children grow up. And as they mature into young adulthood, they bring with them all the baggage of feelings caused by their neglect and abuse situations. They require help in sorting through their feelings and learning how to cope with the experience of abuse and abandonment.

They also need to learn all those things which are necessary in order to live on their own—how to buy, store, and prepare food; how to rent an apartment and open a checking account; how to establish credit; how to find a good job, apply for it, and relate to employers and other workers on the job. There are also many health issues—getting medical insurance, disease prevention, birth control, consequences of drug and alcohol abuse.

There are so many things that foster children need to know as they prepare to be on their own. For many, the prospect of independence is strongly desired but it is also frightening and a source of great anxiety. As foster children face the inevitable day when they are totally, completely on their own, foster parents and staff must work to prepare them. At the same time, we must let them know that we have confidence in their ability to do well, and we will help them connect with people who can provide continued support.

"IT'S NOT MY FAULT THEY LEFT"—GEORGE

George had been abandoned at 12 years of age and had gone through many years of "acting out" his anger. A sympathetic counselor helped him to understand this anger, and to accept his mother as a person who had overwhelming personal problems that prevented her from giving him the love and care that a child deserves.

George will probably, however, continue to struggle with issues of loss and abandonment. As we move through the various stages of our lives, we must all re-work the unfinished business, the unreconciled feelings that we sometimes think we have left behind.

> *[My counselor] helped me out better because she knew…I was mainly mad all the time because I didn't have a mother. I actually did have a mother; I just didn't have my biological mother. I had my foster mother, Jean, but she wasn't the same.*
>
> *My counselor taught me to accept Jean as my mother figure. She is my mother now. That's all I'm going to have.*
>
> *When I was in elementary school, I really didn't have too many friends, probably because of my bad attitude. I would say I always thought negative about my life. Now it's like, think positive. I just really grew up within the last two years of my life.*
>
> *I still have problems to deal with, but I got over some of them. I finally accepted my mother abandoning us. One of the major reasons I had problems was because I had not accepted it. Real close to that time period I moved over to Jean's house. My sister went to college. Then she abandoned us as well. She*

dropped [out of] college and went to Missouri. Then I started dealing with that.

Everybody in my life, all my relatives, don't care about me. They would rather me be dead than alive, just because they don't associate with me anyway. They didn't want me when I was a kid, so why would they want me now? Then I thought, well, maybe it's better for me to be here. My mom abandoned me—well her abandoning me may turn out to be positive. It has turned out to be positive, because if I was with her, Lord knows where I would be, probably in a dump somewhere. Or I could be dead by now because she abandoned me and my two sisters.

I really had a lot of problems when I was a kid, because my mom left and my older sister left and my dad didn't want me. I realize they weren't financially secure, they weren't financially able to support us at the time, and they're probably still not. But that's not my fault they left. They left for their own reasons. They didn't want us for their own reasons.

A lot of people should realize that it is important to live life to the fullest. Accept your relatives for who they are, take God into your life and live life to the fullest.

"Being on my own scares me"—Lance

As Lance prepared to graduate from high school and go on to college, he was unsure about his ability to handle all the freedom he was going to have. It seemed frightening to realize that he would soon have no one but himself to answer to, and he wasn't certain that he was ready for this:

> *The thing that scares me the most about being on my own is the fact that being in college classes is not mandatory. If I want to stay up to 3 a.m. partying, what's going to stop me? I'm disciplined in some areas, but in other areas, I don't know.*
>
> *But as far as being on my own, that scares me kinda. I'm going to need to make some of my own meals, I'm going to need to do things, you know. It's kinda like, I don't know if I'm ready. I might be, I might not. A lot of times if I look at everything I*

know how to do, I feel better. I can cook; I can throw together relatively cheap meals if I want; I can budget; and I can do my laundry.

But when I think about being on my own, I don't feel confident and prepared. I haven't really had the liberty to jump on the phone whenever I want and do other things whenever I want. Right now, I have almost that much freedom, but it's not just me and whatever I want to do is fine. I'm going to be 18 a little bit after I go to college. Decisions are gonna be up to me. I'll think —wow—I can do things now…I hope I will make the right choices.

"I'LL HAVE TO BE READY, BUT I'M STILL SCARED"
—ADRIANNE

As Adrianne faced the day of graduation from high school and termination from foster care, she became very anxious about facing life on her own. Fortunately, she was able to move to a special program designed to help girls prepare for independence:

> Let me put it this way. There's a thing of being ready, and knowing you're ready. Now being ready, I'm sorta there. And knowing you're ready, it doesn't matter who you are, you're always gonna be scared. I've learned more here about moving out and becoming independent than I have anywhere else. And I spent four years in the other home.
>
> You know, if I had stayed there, I would not have known what I know now. I would never have had a savings account, ever. I wouldn't know how to rent an apartment and all those kinds of things. I didn't know that until I came here. I now know that no matter what, I'll have to be ready. I know a lot more than I used to, but I'm still scared.

"SHE TAUGHT ME HOW TO LIVE ON MY OWN"—SAM

Sam's foster mother and caseworker worked as a team to help him prepare to be on his own. They both knew, however, that Sam would need ongoing support and encouragement and told him that they were there for him for that need:

> *[My caseworker at Pathway] helped me out. She would get information I needed for certain things. If I needed to know something about a college, or the Air Force, or something like that, she would do her best to find it out.*
>
> *She and Jean [foster mother] both worked together to help me learn how to be on my own. Jean would teach me how to cook and my caseworker would teach me about the expenses. Jean also rented out apartments. She still does. I kind of had an idea of how much an apartment costs, what all you have to pay for in an apartment. But I never really understood that until a couple of weeks before I moved. My caseworker helped me out on that one, too. She helped me with my living arrangements, which involved where I would be living after I moved out of Jean's house or after I turned 18. She did teach me a lot about how to live independently on my own.*

"I'm not old enough"—Robyn

As she talked to me, Robyn reflected the deep-down fear and anxiety she felt over being on her own. In saying she didn't think she was "old enough" to be going to college, she was talking about a wish that she could be back in her foster home, still dependent:

> *Mostly it was the Independent Living Books. Those things bothered me to no end. There was some stuff in there that was kind of cheesy and kind of like common sense. But some of it in there kind of made me think that I wasn't ready to have to learn these things. I always feel like I am younger than I am. I don't think that I am necessarily going to college. I am not old enough.*
>
> *My foster mom kind of got me into starting a bank account, saving money, doing the things that grown up people do, such as getting my license, paying insurance and all that stuff. She would also be there, like, 'It's all right. It will get better—I promise.' She was really good about it.*

These youth are expressing both their desire to be independent, and their fears of not being able to make it own their own. Foster parents who can validate fears as well as hopes about independence are providing a very important service to these youth. It is also helpful for foster parents to continue to support the youth in whatever ways possible, because we all need supportive people in our lives.

"FAMILY TREE" was drawn by an 8-year-old girl. She shows a comfortable bed to shelter her, and places all of the "good people" close to her in the tree. She places a "bad person" on a lower branch.

Chapter 7
Advice to Foster Parents

One of the questions I asked of every child I interviewed was, "What would you tell foster parents if you were in charge of providing their training?"

Their answers reflected their experiences. For example, one youth had lived in a home that he experienced as cold and unfeeling. He felt the foster parent was only doing this because of the money that she was receiving for his care. When I asked him how he felt about this, he replied in one terse word, "Used." His advice to foster parents was, "If you're going to be a foster parent, don't be in it for the money."

Many of the other youth spoke of the need for foster parents to listen. Children—foster children as well as birth children—often have the experience of feeling their parents do not listen to them. For some, this is a deep-down sense of being discounted or not being valued. It takes a lot of work for foster parents to not only listen, but also to make sure that children know they are being listened to.

Perhaps you have had the experience of having a problem. The problem eats at you, creating tension and frustration. The problem seems so big and powerful that you know you will never be able to cope with it. You feel isolated and alone, like no one in the world has ever had a problem like this.

If, however, you have been able to go with your problem to a person who really, truly listens to you, without judging you or telling you what to do, just hearing what you say as you express yourself, then you know the relief that comes because of having been listened to. Suddenly, the problem does not seem so large. You know that other people have experienced this, and with support, have survived. And you know that you can too.

One of the best ways in which we can communicate love to children is to really listen to them. Sometimes this means listening to what is not being said, as well as to what is being said. Sometimes it means "listening to behavior," understanding what the child may be saying by the way he is acting. Successful foster parents are always good listeners.

Other foster children spoke with me about the need for foster parents to be "patient" and "let the kids make some mistakes." Many foster children live with the daily fear of being "thrown out" of their foster homes because of some action they have taken. The foster children I spoke with counseled that there is a great need for foster parents to be flexible, to remember what it was like to be a child or teenager, and to allow for a few mistakes on the part of children.

TARA, AGE 15, SAID:

> *Include foster children in whatever your plans are. Make them always feel wanted and comfortable. You have to get to know them and how they feel. And you also need to spend quality*

time one-on-one with them.

ERIN, AGE 17 SAID:

> Just take time out, you know. Tell 'em that you love 'em from time to time, because sometimes these foster kids don't really hear that much their whole life. They may not have heard that word before, and that makes a lot of difference, let me tell you.
>
> You want to make them feel like they're a part of your family and that's really important, I think, because every child needs to belong somewhere, within a family. It just makes a child like an outsider, if you exclude him from your family. I'm not talking about taking them on 20 vacations with you, but the things you do, include them with you, you know.
>
> It really makes a difference, because most foster children think that, you know, they are there just to eat, sleep, and do whatever. When you include a foster child in family activities, it helps them. I think it helps a lot. And it makes them feel loved. Even if you just go to a park or something, it's a family event or maybe you have a picnic. It's really helpful, I think.

KAREN, AGE 18 SAID:

> The only thing that I can say is to listen to what they have to say and take it into thought. Don't just sit down and listen and then blow it off. It does not work that way.
>
> Just talk to them about how they are feeling and like when they first move in, try and find out how you can help them when they get mad or if they are upset or something like that. Comfort them a lot because I know from personal experience that when children first come into the system, they are hurting. I mean they are really hurting.
>
> You should come home and talk to them. Let them know that they are a part of the family and that you would do anything possible to help them and stuff like that. That's what my foster mom did with me when I first moved in. We would just sit down and have long talks.

JOHN, AGE 15 SAID:

> Well, I mean, you just gotta be there for the kid, you know. You're not gonna get a kid who's perfect and doesn't have problems. You're gonna have to deal with it. Just 'cause he won't take out the garbage you're not gonna say, we don't want him in our house anymore. You gotta learn how to deal with it and get through it without getting angry all the time. You gotta be someone who enjoys kids, 'cause otherwise it's not gonna work out.

SALINA, AGE 19 SAID:

> I'd tell them to let the kids screw up, but don't tear 'em apart for doing it. I think that if people didn't make mistakes, they wouldn't learn anything in life. And I think you have to make mistakes to learn anything.
>
> And listen, because a lot of times people won't want to listen to younger kids, and I struggled with that. Nobody ever cared what I had to say, because I was the delinquent teenager. I was a juvenile delinquent. And, you know, I think listening, being open-minded, and having emotional affection with the child will make it a lot easier. And don't forget what it was like to be a kid. I think that's probably what I would have to tell them.

RUTH ANN, AGE 18 SAID:

> I would tell them to try and be patient. There is a lot of things that every child has to work through on their own. It's not going to help by being angry with them or frustrated or getting over-emotional about the whole thing. I would tell them to just slow down. If the child needs to vent, then let them. If they need to scream, then let them. I know some parents that get really crazy about that. They hate it when children do that. But sometimes that's just what they need.
>
> I would tell them definitely to let them get out their anger and to get out their emotions and not kind of hold it against them. I would tell them to just be patient.

SARAH, AGE 21 SAID:

> The staff should listen to their clients and the foster parents should always listen to their kids. If the foster parents feel the children have a problem, don't just ask them and just give up on it if they say no. Keep on bugging them, and eventually it will come out.
>
> A lot of times I noticed that when I was angry, I was acting out in a lot of different ways. I wouldn't talk. I wasn't talking to the person for a long time, and I would just act out. A lot of times nobody would ask me what was wrong. It was just like they don't care, so I'll just go do this and they will be mad at me, but at least I'll get some attention. I've noticed that same thing with a lot of other kids. Instead of talking about their problems, they just act out.
>
> Other times you should just listen to the kids. I think that's about the most important, and just love them.

LEON, AGE 17 SAID:

> As far as foster parents, I think the selection is more what makes the foster parent. I know that when you're interviewing the people, they can act however they want. It's not like you guys are selecting bad people on purpose. But I think it is important for staff to keep checking up on foster parents.
>
> I also think the parents should be more open with the kids, you know? They should let the kids know what they expect. I think like within the first week kids should understand the rules and understand why the parents say what they say. Like if I didn't know that they want me home by 9 p.m. for my safety, I think they just want me home by nine to ruin my life. People choose to look at things completely differently. What means one thing to me, means something completely different to you.
>
> And I think that in that type of situation, differences should be explained. Like if a foster child wants to say something to the foster parent, that child should be able to say it. The child shouldn't be rude or whatever.

And the parents should have a time where they're just going to be open with the kids and the kids can be open with them... The parents should have a time where everybody's together and explaining things. But at the end they should also say 'If anyone wants to ask me anything, they can.' Or if you want to talk about something in private, or express feelings about anything... it should be like that, just to keep communication open...

You can't judge people. If you start judging somebody, you're gonna ruin the relationship. If parents start judging kids, it doesn't work. If kids start judging the parents, it doesn't work. When you start judging people, nothing works. So if people just leave other people alone, and if I have a problem with you, let's discuss it instead of me judging and then choosing to have such and such an attitude toward you because you did whatever... Yes, it's hard not to judge people, but... you have to learn sometime.

SHARON, AGE 15 SAID:

" *I'd probably say something like... When we go to foster parents, it seems like [sometimes] they don't understand that we've already been through a lot of stuff in our life, and we don't want even more turmoil. We want you to help our lives, put us on the right path, don't push us off. Some people act like they don't care. They don't understand that we've already been through a lot of stuff, we've already been through a lot of pain, so why should we come to your house and suffer more pain?*

The reflections and viewpoints we have heard in this chapter are a starting point. Hopefully, we will find positive and helpful responses to some of the ideas and suggestions offered by Tara, Karen, John, Salina, Ruth Ann, Sarah and Sharon. And of course, it's not only foster parents, but anyone who really cares, who can learn from what these young people are telling us.

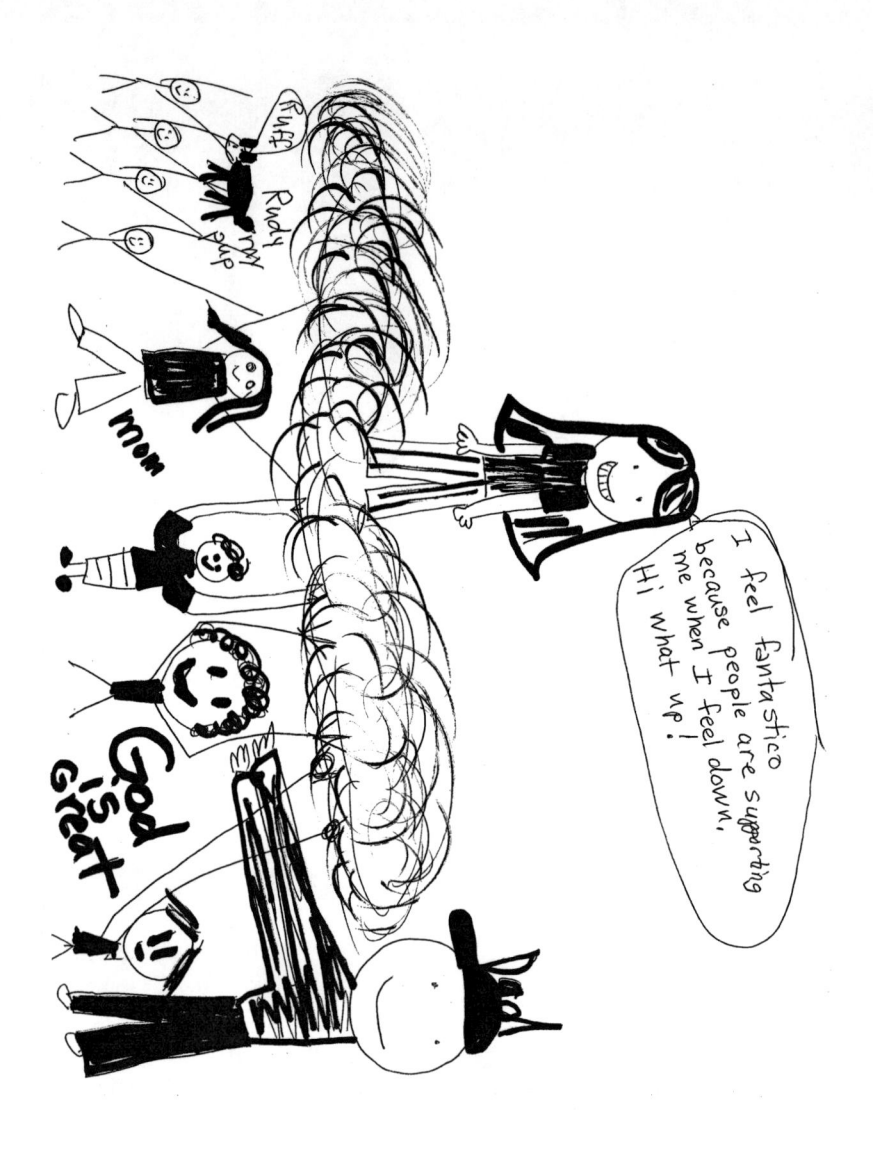

"I FEEL FANTASTICO BECAUSE PEOPLE ARE SUPPORTING ME WHEN I FEEL DOWN" was drawn by Justina and Latrice Schlabaugh, who are 11 and 9 years old.

Chapter 8
Hope For the Future

Although my late husband, Jim Bridges, talked with the foster children quoted in this book a number of years ago, the things these youth have said are still relevant today. We currently face many challenges in the child welfare field. Needs are great. More and more children have been trapped in the self-perpetuating cycle of rejection, negative self-image and antisocial behavior. Problems such as unemployment, extreme poverty, mental illness and drug and alcohol addiction continue to victimize vulnerable children. Resources are limited. There is a shortage of foster and adoptive families. Public funding of child welfare services has been reduced.

Now more than ever, we need to listen to the voices of Heather and Herman, Salina and Sam, as they share with us from their experiences—as they talk about what has helped and what has hurt them. More than ever, we need to learn how to respond to them with respect and compassion. We need to break the cycle of despair.

Some of the youth quoted in this book have clearly expressed the pain of rejection. "I felt like nobody wanted me; that I was just like nothing to anyone…" Other youth tell about their joy when they are welcomed into a home and included in family activities. "This family understood me and helped me feel comfortable. It wasn't like 'Oh, no! Here comes another child.' It was like, 'I'm taking care of another child. I'm helping somebody out.' Making a difference, you know, in her life."

The youth quoted in this book also have a lot to say about agency staff and families who have made a difference in their lives. Certainly listening and working through problems is an important factor. "Well, I mean, for one, helpful foster parents and agency staff members are going to take their time to listen to me. That shows a lot of respect. Then the simple fact that, if we have a problem in the home, it's not, 'We have a problem so get out of the house — we don't want you.' They're gonna work through it until we get it solved."

A number of youth talk about the importance of foster caregivers letting their children know that they care. "Just take time out, you know. Tell 'em that you love 'em from time to time, because sometimes these foster kids don't really hear that much their whole life. They may not have heard that word before, and that makes a lot of difference, let me tell you."

Patience and understanding that foster children have already suffered significant emotional pain is also very important if we want to make a difference as one youth advised. "I would tell foster parents to try and be patient. There are a lot of things that every child has to work through on their own. It's not going to help by being angry with them or frustrated or getting over-emotional about the whole thing."

Another youth advised foster parents to spend quality time with foster children and include them in family activities. "Include foster children in whatever your plans are. Make them always feel wanted and comfortable. You have to get to know them and how they feel. And you also need to spend quality time one-on-one with them."

In addition, it is important for staff members and foster parents to work together to teach youth the skills needed for future success. "My caseworker and Jean [foster mother] both worked together to help me learn how to be on my own. Jean would teach me how to cook and my caseworker would teach me about the expenses."

And so, as we look to the future, the challenge for all of us is to truly listen to these children and all the children we serve—and to learn from them. Ideally, agency staff, foster parents, adoptive parents, and everyone who comes into contact with these children will see them through a lens of love and compassion.

In Chapter One, Jim talks about good news. He has seen positive results when foster and adoptive parents are prepared and supported. He has seen children blossom when they are accepted for who they are, helped to see themselves as persons of worth, and shown how to succeed in school, work, social and family relationships.

"The negative cycle can be broken. It has happened and will happen again in the lives of many, many children."

The challenge is great. There are many ways to participate. Of course, therapists, case managers, and foster and adoptive parents are needed. But anyone who cares about children who have suffered abuse, neglect, and/or abandonment can help. Our children and their foster/adoptive families need advocates, mentors, respite providers and other supportive services. Agencies need financial contributions in order to provide the services these children and families need and deserve. There is something for everyone to do.

Together we can make a real and lasting difference in the lives of these vulnerable children.

Tribute to the Author
Jim Bridges, Founder and Executive Director of Pathway Caring for Children from 1973 to 2009.

My late husband, Jim Bridges, dedicated his life to making a difference in the lives of children, especially foster children. He began to see the need for effective child welfare services while he was growing up. Jim's father had experienced abuse, neglect and abandonment as a child. As Jim says, "Out of the experience of watching my father grapple with the demons of hurt, anger, and distrust bequeathed to him by years of abuse and neglect, has come a commitment in me to prevent that from happening in the lives of the children of today."

Many years later, after college and graduate school, Jim was working as a caseworker in a public foster care agency. Jim and the other caseworkers had little training and caseloads as large as 80 children. Foster parents also had little training and support. As a result, these foster parents were sometimes unable to meet the needs of the children placed in their homes. Jim wrote the following: "It wasn't long before I realized that I was constantly putting children on a foster care merry-go-round, moving them from foster home to foster home, over and over again. It was only making things worse. 'There has to be a better way,' I told myself. And that thought was the beginning of Pathway Caring for Children."

Several years later, Jim's vision became a reality when the first four boys were placed in the first Pathway group home. In a few years, Pathway began training, licensing and supporting foster parents to provide care for children with special needs. Under Jim's leadership, adoption, post adoption and mental health services were also added in order to improve continuity of services and the quality of care for children and families in need.

Jim's life and his work were guided by seven ideals stated in the Values Statement of Pathway Caring for Children. At Pathway, we seek to carry out seven basic ideals with the youth who come to us. Most important, we *love* and care for each youth individually. We *recognize* them as persons of worth and teach them to *respect* themselves and others; provide them with the *security* of knowing that we are there for them; help them find the paths of *success* in school, work and social relationships; encourage them in the assumption of *responsibility* for themselves and their actions; and become *personally involved* with them in their struggle for meaning and purpose in life.